Navigating Challenges in High Society

C. P. Kumar
Reiki Healer
Roorkee - 247667, India

Disclaimer

While every effort has been made to ensure the accuracy and completeness of the content in this book, the author cannot guarantee that the information contained herein is error-free, up-to-date, or suitable for every individual circumstance.

The author shall not be held liable or responsible for any errors or omissions in the content of the book, nor for any damages, or losses that may arise from any actions taken based upon the suggestions or contents presented in the book.

Readers are advised to use their own judgment and discretion in applying the information provided in this book, and to consult with qualified professionals before taking any action based on the contents of this book. The author disclaims any and all liability or responsibility for any actions taken or not taken based on the information contained in this book.

DEDICATION

To all those who reside within the gilded halls of high society, yet recognize the complexities of privilege and the profound challenges it poses.

May this book serve as a guiding light through the intricate web of societal expectations, material excess, and the relentless pursuit of perfection.

In the pursuit of a more balanced and fulfilling existence, may you find inspiration within these pages to navigate the intricacies of high-class living with wisdom, compassion, and a commitment to positive change.

This book is dedicated to the courageous souls who dare to transform their world, embracing mindfulness, forging genuine connections, and redefining success in the noble pursuit of a better society for all.

C. P. Kumar

CONTENTS

PREFACE

In the grand theater of life, there exists a tier above the ordinary, a realm often veiled in opulence and glamour, known as high society. It's a world where wealth and prestige converge, where luxury is not a privilege but a way of life. Yet, beyond the shimmering facade, beneath the veneer of sophistication, lies a paradoxical tapestry of challenges and dilemmas that remain concealed from the casual observer.

"Navigating Challenges in High Society" embarks on a journey through the intricate web of this exclusive realm, unveiling the unique problems that beset those who dwell within its gilded walls. This book is an exploration of the hidden undercurrents beneath the glittering surface, an invitation to confront the realities and complexities of high-class society that often remain unspoken.

As we delve into these pages, we will navigate the turbulent waters of wealth disparities and inequities that silently fracture the very foundation of this society. We will dissect the corrosive impact of materialism and consumerism on the well-being of its inhabitants and, by extension, on society as a whole. We will peer behind the facade of social isolation and loneliness that accompanies the high-class lifestyle, illuminating the shadows of mental health struggles and the unrelenting burden of unrealistic expectations.

But this is not a mere exposé of challenges; it is a compass for transformation. Throughout this journey, we shall not only dissect the problems but also propose solutions. We will redefine success, shifting the focus from material acquisitions to holistic well-being, personal growth, and meaningful connections. We will explore the significance of ethical considerations, social responsibility, and giving back to society. We will champion sustainable living, urging a departure from extravagant waste to environmentally conscious choices.

From the intricate dynamics of high-class families to the profound work-life imbalance, from the quest for authenticity in relationships to the pursuit of genuine happiness, we endeavor to uncover the myriad facets of a lifestyle often misunderstood. In this pursuit, we shall promote mindfulness and well-being, offer strategies for creating a balanced lifestyle, and provide the tools to foster meaningful, lasting relationships.

This book is more than a guide; it is a call to action. It is an appeal to high-class society to redefine its values, reassess its priorities, and embrace a future where prosperity is not measured solely by wealth but by the well-being of individuals and the sustainability of our planet. It is an invitation to reflect, to act, and to be part of a movement that envisions a high society where responsibility, compassion, and mindfulness shine as brightly as the chandeliers in its grandest ballrooms.

So, as we embark on this exploration of high-class society, let us prepare to navigate the challenges, confront the dilemmas, and emerge as architects of change. For within the rarified air of this world, there lies not just privilege but the potential for profound transformation. Welcome to a journey that transcends the superficial and embraces the profound. Welcome to "Navigating Challenges in High Society".

C. P. Kumar
Reiki Healer
Former Scientist 'G', National Institute of Hydrology
Roorkee - 247667, India
Web: https://www.angelfire.com/nh/cpkumar/virgo.html

Introduction

High-class society, often associated with wealth, privilege, and prestige, is often seen as a realm of opulence and luxury. However, beneath the facade of lavish lifestyles and social standing, high-class society members face a unique set of challenges and issues that are often overlooked. In this article, we will provide a brief overview of the challenges faced by the high-class society, emphasizing the need to address these issues. "Navigating Challenges in High Society" is a book dedicated to shedding light on these concerns and offering potential solutions.

1. The Pressure to Maintain Status

In high-class society, there is an immense pressure to maintain one's social standing. This pressure can lead to a constant state of stress and anxiety. People in these circles often feel compelled to conform to certain standards and expectations, whether in terms of their appearance, social interactions, or even career choices. The fear of losing one's status can be overwhelming, leading to a variety of mental and emotional challenges.

2. Isolation and Loneliness

Surprisingly, high-class society can be an incredibly lonely place. Individuals in these circles often find it difficult to form genuine connections with others, as many relationships are superficial or driven by mutual interests. Moreover, the fear of betrayal and exploitation can further isolate high-class society members, making it difficult for them to trust others.

3. The Impact of Scandals and Public Scrutiny

High-class society is no stranger to scandals and public scrutiny. The media and the public often closely follow the lives of high-profile individuals, waiting for any misstep or controversy. The consequences of such scandals can be far-reaching, affecting not only the individual but also their family and social standing. This constant fear of being exposed can lead to high levels of stress and anxiety.

4. High Expectations and Perfectionism

High-class society members are often held to incredibly high standards. The need to maintain a perfect image can be psychologically taxing. It can lead to a relentless pursuit of perfection and an inability to accept any form of failure. This pressure can lead to anxiety, depression, and a range of other mental health issues.

5. Family Dynamics and Inheritance Issues

Inheritance and family wealth are often significant concerns in high-class society. Family dynamics can be complex, with disputes over wealth distribution and the inheritance of family businesses. These issues can lead to rifts within families and create a sense of insecurity among the younger generations, who may feel the pressure of living up to their family's legacy.

6. Dependence on Material Possessions

The high-class society often revolves around material possessions and the pursuit of wealth. This obsession with materialism can lead to a shallow and unfulfilling life. It can be challenging for individuals to find meaning and purpose beyond their wealth and possessions, which can result in a lack of satisfaction and a sense of emptiness.

7. Lack of Privacy

High-class society individuals often find themselves with little to no privacy. Constant media attention, social events, and public appearances can make it challenging to lead a private and peaceful life. The lack of personal space and the feeling of being constantly under the spotlight can be emotionally taxing.

8. Mental Health Stigma

There is often a stigma associated with mental health issues in high-class society. Seeking help for mental health problems is seen as a sign of weakness, and individuals may hesitate to access the support they need. This stigma can prevent them from addressing their mental health concerns, leading to further emotional distress.

9. Charity and Social Responsibility

Members of high-class society often face pressure to be involved in charitable activities and social responsibility initiatives. While this is a positive aspect, it can also become a burden when individuals feel obligated to engage in these activities, often out of fear of losing social status or facing criticism for not contributing to society.

10. Entitlement and Arrogance

High-class society can sometimes foster a sense of entitlement and arrogance. Individuals may develop a superiority complex, believing that they are above others due to their social standing and wealth. This attitude can lead to strained relationships and make it difficult for them to relate to individuals from different backgrounds.

The Need to Address High-Class Society Issues

The challenges faced by high-class society members are real and impactful. Ignoring these issues can lead to significant mental and emotional distress, affecting not only individuals but also their families and communities. Addressing these issues is essential for several reasons.

1. Mental Health and Well-Being

Prioritizing mental health and well-being should be a universal goal, regardless of one's social standing. By acknowledging the unique challenges faced by high-class society members, we can work towards destigmatizing mental health issues and encouraging individuals to seek help when needed.

2. Preserving Relationships

Building genuine connections and maintaining healthy relationships is crucial for anyone's happiness and fulfillment. By addressing the challenges of high-class society, we can help individuals in these circles foster more meaningful connections with others.

3. Promoting Social Responsibility

High-class society members have the potential to make a significant positive impact on society. By addressing the issues they face, we can encourage them to channel their resources and influence toward charitable activities and social responsibility initiatives in a more genuine and meaningful way.

4. Reducing Materialism

A focus on material possessions can lead to a shallow and unfulfilling life. By addressing this challenge, we can help individuals in high-class society find meaning and purpose beyond their wealth, leading to greater satisfaction and personal growth.

Conclusion

High-class society may appear glamorous on the surface, but beneath the opulence lies a set of unique challenges that must be acknowledged and addressed. "Navigating Challenges in High Society" is a book dedicated to exploring these issues in greater depth and offering potential solutions. By understanding the pressures, expectations, and vulnerabilities faced by high-class society members, we can work towards creating a more compassionate and inclusive society that values mental health, genuine relationships, and social responsibility, regardless of social standing.

Chapter 2. Wealth Disparities and Inequities

Introduction

The phrase "the rich get richer, and the poor get poorer" is not a new one. Throughout history, societies have grappled with issues of wealth disparity and income inequality. Yet, in recent years, these disparities have taken on new dimensions and have reached alarming levels. This article delves into the multifaceted issue of wealth disparities and inequities, examining the reasons behind the growing wealth gap and income inequality, and exploring the implications for both the high-class and broader society.

The Growing Wealth Gap

The wealth gap refers to the unequal distribution of assets and financial resources among a population. It is important to note that the wealth gap is distinct from income inequality, as wealth encompasses assets such as property, investments, and savings, while income is the money earned through employment or investments.

1. Historical Context

To understand the present wealth gap, it is crucial to recognize its historical roots. Societies have always had varying degrees of wealth inequality. However, the contemporary wealth gap can be traced back to economic policies and systemic changes that have been in motion for several decades.

2. Economic Factors

Several economic factors contribute to the widening wealth gap. One of the most significant is the phenomenon of economic globalization. While globalization has brought about many benefits, such as increased trade and access to global markets, it has also led to greater competition in the workforce, often resulting in wage stagnation for the middle and lower classes.

Additionally, the rise of technology and automation has led to job displacement, with many low-skill and routine jobs being automated. This has created a stark division between those with specialized skills and those without. Those who adapt and acquire in-demand skills often experience greater wealth accumulation, further exacerbating the wealth gap.

3. Taxation and Policy

Taxation policies play a significant role in wealth inequality. In many countries, the wealthy benefit from tax breaks and loopholes, allowing them to preserve and grow their wealth more efficiently. These policies can include lower capital gains taxes, estate tax exemptions, and deductions for mortgage interest on expensive properties.

4. Financial Market Dynamics

The dynamics of the financial market also play a critical role in wealth inequality. The stock market, for instance, has provided significant returns to those who can afford to invest in it. However, not everyone has equal access to the stock market, and the gains accrued disproportionately benefit the already wealthy.

Income Inequality

Income inequality refers to the unequal distribution of earnings among individuals and households. While it is closely related to wealth disparities, it primarily concerns the money people receive from various sources, such as employment, investments, and government assistance.

1. Wage Disparities

One of the most visible aspects of income inequality is the stark contrast in wages. High-income earners, such as corporate executives and top professionals, often earn hundreds of times more than low-wage workers in sectors like retail, hospitality, and agriculture.

2. Gender and Racial Disparities

Income inequality is not uniform; it is compounded by gender and racial disparities. Women, on average, earn less than men for the same work, and minority populations often face additional hurdles in accessing higher-paying jobs and opportunities for advancement.

3. The Gig Economy

The rise of the gig economy has introduced a new dimension to income inequality. While some individuals benefit from the flexibility and higher earnings the gig economy offers, others are trapped in precarious, low-wage work without job security or benefits.

Implications for the High-Class

While it may seem that the high-class benefits from wealth disparities and income inequality, it is essential to recognize that the implications of such disparities are complex and extend beyond simple economic gain.

1. Isolation and Alienation

The high-class often lives in exclusive neighborhoods and social circles, leading to isolation from the broader society. This can result in a lack of empathy and understanding of the challenges faced by those in lower economic strata, potentially contributing to social divisions.

2. Social Responsibility

As wealth increases, so does the potential for social impact. Many high-net-worth individuals recognize their social responsibility and contribute to philanthropic causes, but the effectiveness and accountability of these efforts can vary. Wealthy individuals can exert significant influence on societal issues and, when used thoughtfully, their resources can address some of the disparities they benefit from.

3. Impact on Mental Health

Paradoxically, the high-class can also suffer from the consequences of wealth disparities. The pressures and expectations associated with wealth can lead to mental health issues, including anxiety and depression. The pursuit of maintaining or expanding one's wealth can result in a relentless focus on material success, often at the expense of personal well-being.

Implications for Broader Society

The consequences of wealth disparities and income inequality extend far beyond the high-class, affecting the broader society in numerous ways.

1. Social Cohesion

Extreme wealth inequality can erode social cohesion, as it creates a sense of injustice and unfairness among those left behind. This can lead to social unrest, protests, and even political instability.

2. Opportunity Gaps

Income inequality can exacerbate opportunity gaps, making it more challenging for individuals from lower-income backgrounds to access quality education, healthcare, and job opportunities. This hinders social mobility and perpetuates cycles of poverty.

3. Political Influence

Wealthy individuals and corporations often wield significant political influence, thanks to campaign contributions and lobbying efforts. This influence can result in policies that favor the interests of the wealthy, further entrenching wealth disparities and income inequality.

4. Economic Growth

While some argue that wealth disparities can drive economic growth by incentivizing investment and entrepreneurship, excessive inequality can stifle economic development. It limits the purchasing power of the middle and lower classes, which, in turn, can hinder consumer-driven economies.

Addressing Wealth Disparities and Income Inequality

Addressing wealth disparities and income inequality is a complex and multifaceted challenge. Various strategies can be employed at the individual, societal, and policy levels to mitigate these issues.

1. Progressive Taxation

Implementing progressive taxation policies, where higher-income individuals pay a larger percentage of their income in taxes, can help redistribute wealth and fund social programs that benefit the broader society.

2. Education and Job Training

Investing in education and job training programs can provide individuals with the skills and opportunities needed to access higher-paying jobs, reducing income inequality over time.

3. Fair Wages

Advocating for fair wages, labor rights, and workplace equality can narrow the wage gap and create a more equitable job market.

4. Philanthropy and Social Responsibility

Encouraging the wealthy to engage in strategic philanthropy and socially responsible business practices can channel resources to address societal issues, such as education, healthcare, and poverty.

5. Economic Reforms

Economic reforms that address issues like corporate governance, financial market regulations, and wealth inheritance can help level the playing field and reduce the concentration of wealth.

Conclusion

The growing wealth gap and income inequality are complex issues that have far-reaching implications for both the high-class and broader society. While the high-class may enjoy the benefits of their economic status, they are not immune to the social and mental health consequences that can arise from extreme wealth disparities. For the broader society, income inequality erodes social cohesion, widens opportunity gaps, and influences political decisions.

Addressing these issues requires a concerted effort from individuals, communities, and policymakers. By implementing progressive taxation, investing in education and job training, advocating for fair wages, promoting philanthropy and social responsibility, and enacting economic reforms, we can work towards a more equitable society where wealth and income disparities are less pronounced, and everyone has a fair opportunity to succeed. The challenges posed by these disparities are significant, but the potential benefits of a more equitable society are worth the effort.

Introduction

In our modern world, the pursuit of wealth, status, and luxury has become an overarching goal for many individuals, particularly those in high society. Materialism and consumerism have permeated our culture, influencing our values, priorities, and lifestyles. While these concepts aren't inherently negative, an excessive focus on material possessions and consumption can have profound implications for the well-being of high-class individuals and society as a whole. In this article, we will delve into the complex dynamics of materialism and consumerism, examining their impact on high-class individuals and the broader social fabric.

Understanding Materialism and Consumerism

Before we delve into the impact of materialism and consumerism, it's important to define these terms and understand how they manifest in contemporary society.

Materialism is a value system that places a strong emphasis on the acquisition of material possessions and wealth as a means of achieving happiness and success. It often involves the belief that one's self-worth and identity are closely tied to the possessions they own, leading individuals to accumulate wealth and belongings relentlessly.

Consumerism, on the other hand, is the preoccupation with the acquisition of goods and services in ever-increasing amounts. It encourages individuals to prioritize buying and consuming over other aspects of life, with a focus on the pursuit of the latest trends, brands, and products.

The High-Class Perspective

High-class individuals often find themselves in a unique position when it comes to materialism and consumerism. Their elevated social and economic status provides them with greater access to material goods and luxury, which can exacerbate these tendencies.

1. The Pursuit of Status and Image

High-class individuals often feel pressured to maintain or enhance their status and image within their social circles. This pressure can lead to conspicuous consumption, where individuals buy extravagant items to display their wealth and success. While this may boost their social standing, it can also create a vicious cycle of materialism, where they constantly need to outdo themselves and their peers in terms of possessions.

2. Competitive Consumption

Within high society, competition isn't limited to success in business or careers; it extends to material wealth and consumption. As high-class individuals seek to outdo one another with opulent purchases, they may find themselves trapped in a never-ending cycle of one-upmanship. This competition can lead to financial strain and a diminished sense of well-being.

The Impact on Well-being

Materialism and consumerism can have both personal and societal consequences. It's crucial to explore how these behaviors affect the well-being of high-class individuals and society as a whole.

1. Diminished Psychological Well-being

While high-class individuals may enjoy a level of comfort and luxury, excessive materialism and consumerism can have adverse effects on their psychological well-being. Studies have shown that the relentless pursuit of material wealth and possessions can lead to increased stress, anxiety, and even depression. The pressure to maintain a certain lifestyle and image can be emotionally taxing, creating a constant sense of inadequacy and anxiety.

2. Erosion of Authentic Relationships

Consumerism can also strain interpersonal relationships. When individuals prioritize possessions over people, they may struggle to form and maintain authentic connections with others. High-class individuals may find themselves surrounded by acquaintances and sycophants rather than true friends, further contributing to their sense of isolation and dissatisfaction.

3. Hedonic Adaptation

High-class individuals may experience a phenomenon known as hedonic adaptation, where the pleasure derived from their possessions diminishes over time. This means that they continually seek new, more expensive items to maintain the same level of happiness. In the long run, this adaptation can lead to a never-ending cycle of consumption, as individuals are always in pursuit of the next source of satisfaction.

Societal Implications

Beyond the personal consequences, the influence of materialism and consumerism within high society has far-reaching societal implications.

1. Economic Inequality

Excessive consumerism among the high-class can contribute to economic inequality. When a small portion of the population hoards wealth and resources, it leaves fewer opportunities and resources for the rest of society. This wealth concentration can exacerbate social and economic disparities, leading to social unrest and instability.

2. Environmental Impact

The insatiable appetite for material possessions, particularly in high society, can have a detrimental impact on the environment. The production and disposal of luxury goods often involve the depletion of natural resources and the generation of pollution and waste. The carbon footprint of high-class individuals who engage in frequent international travel and own multiple properties can also be substantial.

3. Emulation and Aspiration

High society often sets trends and standards that are emulated by others in society. As high-class individuals engage in conspicuous consumption, others may aspire to do the same, even if they lack the means to sustain such a lifestyle. This can lead to a culture of debt, where individuals accumulate financial burdens in their pursuit of an unsustainable lifestyle.

Navigating the Challenges

Addressing the challenges posed by materialism and consumerism in high society requires a multi-faceted approach.

1. Self-awareness and Mindfulness

High-class individuals can benefit from cultivating self-awareness and practicing mindfulness. They should reflect on their values, priorities, and the impact of their actions on their well-being and the broader society. Mindfulness can help individuals make more intentional and conscious choices, rather than being driven by societal pressures or impulse buying.

2. Balanced Consumption

Finding a balance between enjoying the benefits of high society and mindful consumption is essential. High-class individuals can appreciate the privileges they have without falling into the trap of excessive materialism. This may involve philanthropy, investing in experiences rather than possessions, and adopting a more minimalist lifestyle.

3. Promoting Responsibility

High society can also play a crucial role in promoting responsible consumerism. By setting positive examples and supporting initiatives that encourage sustainable practices and ethical production, they can mitigate the negative societal impacts of their consumption habits.

4. Reevaluating Success

Reevaluating the definition of success is a fundamental step in addressing materialism and consumerism. High-class individuals should consider whether their happiness and fulfillment are truly linked to the possession of material wealth or if they can find more profound meaning and purpose in other aspects of life, such as relationships, personal growth, and contributions to society.

Conclusion

Materialism and consumerism are complex issues that impact high-class individuals and society at large. The pursuit of wealth, status, and luxury can lead to diminished well-being, strained relationships, and societal challenges. High society must grapple with these challenges and find ways to navigate them effectively.

Ultimately, the path to a more fulfilling and sustainable high-class lifestyle involves self-awareness, balanced consumption, responsible behavior, and a reevaluation of what it means to be successful. By doing so, high-class individuals can not only enhance their own well-being but also contribute to a more equitable and harmonious society.

As high society continues to evolve, addressing the impact of materialism and consumerism remains a pressing concern. It is through thoughtful reflection and responsible action that individuals in high society can foster positive change and set a more inclusive and sustainable example for the world at large.

Introduction

The glitzy world of high society often paints a picture of opulence and exclusivity, with extravagant parties, luxurious lifestyles, and seemingly endless social events. However, beneath the veneer of extravagance lies a troubling reality. Many individuals living high-class lifestyles can experience social isolation and loneliness, which have far-reaching effects on their mental health and relationships. In this article, we will delve into the dynamics of social isolation and loneliness in high society, examining their root causes and the profound impact they can have on the lives of those who seemingly have it all.

The Illusion of Opulence

High society is often perceived as a realm of privilege and abundance, where wealth, status, and glamour converge. Social media, celebrity culture, and glossy magazines portray this lifestyle as a perpetual parade of soirées and gatherings, perpetuating an illusion of constant connection and fulfillment. However, the reality can be starkly different.

1. Superficial Relationships

One of the key challenges in high society is the prevalence of superficial relationships. In such circles, social interactions often revolve around appearances, status, and networking. People may attend gatherings for the sole purpose of being seen and building connections for personal or professional gain. These shallow relationships can leave individuals feeling isolated and empty, as they lack the depth and authenticity required for meaningful connections.

2. FOMO and the Pressure to Socialize

The fear of missing out (FOMO) is a persistent concern in high society. The pressure to be seen at all the right events and gatherings can lead to a frantic socializing schedule. This constant need to be present at high-profile functions can be exhausting and detrimental to one's mental health. Paradoxically, the more events one attends, the less time and energy they have for genuine connections.

The Loneliness Paradox

Loneliness is often mistakenly associated with physical isolation, but it can just as easily occur within a crowd. High society individuals can find themselves surrounded by people yet plagued by feelings of isolation and loneliness.

1. Shallow Connections

Despite the large number of acquaintances and superficial connections, high-society individuals may struggle to find true confidants. Trusting others in a world driven by personal gain can be difficult, making it challenging to form deep, meaningful relationships.

2. Lack of Empathy

Empathy can be scarce in high society, as people are often preoccupied with their own image and status. The absence of genuine empathy can intensify feelings of loneliness, as individuals find themselves yearning for emotional support and understanding.

3. Fear of Vulnerability

Vulnerability is often seen as a sign of weakness in high society. People may hesitate to share their struggles or fears for fear of judgment or social repercussions. This fear of vulnerability can lead to emotional isolation and a sense of loneliness, as individuals keep their true selves hidden behind a facade.

The Impact on Mental Health

Social isolation and loneliness can exact a heavy toll on one's mental health, even in high society. The facade of opulence and success can conceal the hidden pain and suffering of individuals who feel trapped in a world of isolation.

1. Anxiety and Depression

The constant pressure to maintain appearances and socialize can lead to anxiety and depression. The fear of judgment and the weight of expectations can be overwhelming, and many high society individuals experience intense stress and emotional turmoil.

2. Substance Abuse

To cope with their loneliness and emotional struggles, some high society individuals turn to substance abuse, seeking solace in alcohol, drugs, or other vices. This can lead to a dangerous cycle of addiction that further isolates them from loved ones.

3. Burnout

The relentless pursuit of a high-class lifestyle can lead to burnout. The need to be present at social events, maintain a certain image, and continuously network can drain one's physical and emotional resources. This burnout can exacerbate feelings of isolation and exhaustion.

Strained Relationships

Social isolation and loneliness do not just affect individuals; they also have a profound impact on their relationships.

1. Familial Relationships

In high society, family dynamics can become strained due to the demands of maintaining a certain image and constant socializing. Prioritizing personal and professional connections over familial relationships can lead to tensions and estrangement.

2. Romantic Relationships

Romantic relationships can suffer due to the emotional distance and lack of authenticity that often plague high society interactions. The constant need to appear perfect can create an emotional barrier, making it difficult for partners to connect on a deep level.

3. Friendships

Loneliness can erode existing friendships and hinder the formation of new ones. High society individuals may struggle to find friends who truly understand their experiences and emotions, leaving them feeling isolated even within their social circles.

Coping Strategies and Solutions

Navigating the challenges of social isolation and loneliness in high society is possible, but it requires a conscious effort to break free from the superficiality that often defines this world.

1. Authenticity

High society individuals can begin by striving for authenticity in their interactions. Building genuine connections based on mutual trust and respect can provide a foundation for meaningful relationships.

2. Self-Care

Prioritizing self-care is essential for combating the mental health challenges associated with high society. Taking time for oneself, seeking therapy, and practicing mindfulness can help individuals cope with stress and anxiety.

3. Redefining Success

Reevaluating the definition of success is crucial. Success does not have to be solely about wealth and status. High society individuals can find fulfillment in personal growth, creativity, and helping others.

4. Breaking the Mold

High society individuals can challenge the status quo by being open about their struggles and vulnerabilities. By doing so, they may inspire others to do the same, creating a more supportive and empathetic social environment.

5. Balance

Balancing social commitments and personal time is key to combating burnout and isolation. Learning to say no and focusing on quality over quantity in relationships can lead to a more fulfilling social life.

Conclusion

Social isolation and loneliness can cast a shadow over the glamorous world of high society. The superficiality, fear of vulnerability, and pressure to conform to societal expectations can lead to a profound sense of emptiness. However, individuals in high society have the power to change their own narrative by prioritizing authenticity, self-care, and meaningful relationships. Navigating the challenges of loneliness and isolation in high society may be a complex journey, but it is a path towards a happier, more fulfilling life.

By acknowledging the hidden struggles within high society, individuals can work toward building a community that values empathy, connection, and genuine relationships. Only then can they truly enjoy the privileges that come with a high-class lifestyle without succumbing to the isolation and loneliness that often accompany it.

Introduction

In our modern world, high society often revels in opulence and excess, with extravagant parties, luxurious travel, and lavish possessions defining the lifestyle of the elite. While such extravagance may be alluring, it is essential to recognize that these indulgences come at a significant environmental cost. The consequences of lavish lifestyles, characterized by excessive resource consumption and waste production, are far-reaching, impacting not only the planet but also the very society that perpetuates them. This article delves into the environmental effects of opulent living, exploring how they contribute to global challenges like climate change, resource depletion, and waste crisis.

The Carbon Footprint of Luxury Travel

1. Private Jets and Superyachts

High society often boasts of its ability to travel the world in style, frequently opting for private jets and superyachts as modes of transportation. While these are symbols of status and privilege, they also leave a massive carbon footprint. Private jets emit a significant amount of greenhouse gases per passenger compared to commercial flights. Superyachts, often equipped with luxurious amenities, consume vast quantities of fuel. The carbon emissions from these modes of travel contribute to the overall problem of climate change, accelerating global warming and its associated effects.

Elite travelers frequently stay in luxury resorts that are energy-intensive. These establishments often prioritize aesthetics and opulence over sustainability. The massive energy consumption of such resorts, whether it's for climate control, lighting, or other amenities, places an additional burden on the environment. High society's preference for energy-intensive accommodations directly contributes to higher energy demands and associated emissions.

The Resource Intensive Nature of Lavish Lifestyles

1. Fast Fashion and Excessive Clothing Consumption

Fashion is a hallmark of high society, with individuals often seen in the latest designer outfits. However, the fast-paced nature of the fashion industry and the constant demand for new trends contribute to resource depletion. The production of clothing, particularly fast fashion, consumes vast amounts of water, energy, and raw materials. Furthermore, the disposal of old, unwanted garments generates enormous waste, contributing to landfills and environmental pollution.

2. High-End Automobiles and Their Resource Requirements

Luxury cars are a symbol of prestige in high society, but they come at an environmental cost. The production of high-end automobiles involves extensive resource consumption, from the extraction of metals and minerals for manufacturing to the energy required in the production process. These vehicles also consume more fuel, contributing to increased greenhouse gas emissions. The overall resource-intensive nature of the automotive industry in high society exacerbates global resource depletion.

3. Extravagant Home Building and the Impact on Land and Resources

High society often builds opulent homes that are spacious and equipped with the latest technology and amenities. These homes typically occupy large plots of land and consume substantial resources in their construction. The preference for extravagant residences leads to deforestation, habitat destruction, and increased demand for materials like wood and stone, placing additional strain on natural resources.

The Waste Crisis in High Society

1. Excessive Packaging and Single-Use Products

The affluent often prioritize convenience and aesthetics in their purchases, leading to excessive packaging and the use of single-use products. These practices result in significant waste generation, as luxury goods come with elaborate packaging that is discarded after use. Moreover, single-use items like plastic cutlery, straws, and containers are prevalent in high society, contributing to the plastic pollution crisis.

2. Food Waste and Extravagant Dining

Fine dining is a common pursuit in high society, but it often leads to food waste. Expensive meals are often characterized by multiple courses, elaborate presentations, and oversized portions. This results in a considerable amount of food being discarded, contributing to the global food waste problem.

3. The Disposal of Outdated Electronics and Gadgets

High society frequently adopts the latest technology and gadgets, discarding older devices. The disposal of outdated electronics, which often contain hazardous materials, poses a significant environmental threat. Improper electronic waste disposal can lead to soil and water contamination, contributing to the growing e-waste crisis.

The Consequences of Lavish Lifestyles

1. Accelerating Climate Change

The carbon emissions from private jets, superyachts, and energy-intensive luxury resorts are substantial contributors to climate change. High society's travel and accommodation choices have a direct impact on global warming, increasing the frequency and severity of extreme weather events and jeopardizing ecosystems.

2. Depletion of Natural Resources

The resource-intensive nature of high-end fashion, automobile production, and extravagant home building contributes to the depletion of natural resources. As the elite continue to prioritize luxury and opulence, the strain on the planet's resources intensifies, making them scarcer and more expensive for everyone.

3. Exacerbating the Waste Crisis

The waste generated by lavish lifestyles, including excessive packaging, food waste, and the disposal of outdated electronics, worsens the ongoing waste crisis. As landfills overflow and oceans become increasingly polluted, these practices have long-term repercussions for the environment and future generations.

Sustainable Practices in High Society

To address the environmental consequences of lavish lifestyles, it is imperative that high society embraces sustainable practices. This involves a shift in mindset and behavior, recognizing that opulence should not come at the expense of the planet. Here are some steps that the elite can take:

Eco-Friendly Travel: Opt for more sustainable modes of transportation, such as commercial flights or electric cars. Additionally, support companies that are investing in greener technologies for private jets and superyachts.

Sustainable Fashion: Embrace ethical and sustainable fashion brands that prioritize eco-friendly materials and ethical production processes. Buy fewer, high-quality items that stand the test of time.

Green Building Practices: Choose sustainable building materials and energy-efficient technology when constructing luxurious homes. Prioritize sustainable architecture and design that minimizes the environmental impact.

Reduce Waste: Minimize packaging and single-use products in daily life. Support restaurants and catering services that emphasize portion control and food waste reduction. Recycle and responsibly dispose of electronic waste.

Philanthropy and Environmental Initiatives

High society holds a unique position of influence and wealth, and they can harness their resources to support environmental causes. Philanthropic efforts can contribute significantly to mitigating the consequences of lavish lifestyles. These efforts include:

Investing in Conservation: High-profile individuals can invest in and support conservation projects aimed at preserving natural habitats, protecting endangered species, and combating deforestation.

Supporting Environmental Education: Funding programs and initiatives that promote environmental education can help raise awareness and inspire change within high society.

Promoting Sustainable Innovation: Support research and development of eco-friendly technologies and practices that can be adopted on a broader scale.

Advocating for Policy Change: Use their influence to advocate for policies and regulations that promote sustainability and environmental protection.

Leading by Example

High society figures can set a powerful example for the world by adopting sustainable practices in their own lives. By showcasing eco-friendly choices and embracing a greener way of living, they can inspire their peers and followers to do the same.

Conclusion

The environmental impact of lavish lifestyles in high society is undeniable. Excessive resource consumption, carbon emissions from luxury travel, and waste generation pose significant challenges for our planet. However, there is an opportunity for change. By embracing sustainable practices, supporting environmental initiatives, and leading by example, the elite of society can play a vital role in mitigating these consequences. The shift towards eco-conscious living not only benefits the environment but also ensures a more sustainable and responsible high society for generations to come. Navigating the challenges of opulence and privilege demands a commitment to the well-being of the planet and all its inhabitants.

Introduction

In the glittering world of high society, where opulence and privilege often seem to reign supreme, it's easy to assume that life is a never-ending parade of lavish parties, elegant soirees, and extravagant vacations. Yet, beneath the façade of glamour and privilege, high-class individuals grapple with their fair share of mental health struggles. In this article, we will delve into the complex and often hidden world of mental health issues faced by those living in high society. We will explore how stress, anxiety, and the relentless pressure to maintain appearances can take a toll on their well-being, and offer insights into navigating these unique challenges.

The Pressure to Appear Perfect

High-class individuals often find themselves in the spotlight, scrutinized by both the media and their peers. The expectation to maintain an image of perfection can be overwhelming and contribute to a range of mental health issues.

1. Unrealistic Expectations

The constant pressure to appear flawless in every aspect of life can lead to unrealistic expectations. High-class individuals may feel compelled to have perfect bodies, immaculate homes, and impeccable social lives. Such pressure can create an immense burden, causing anxiety and self-esteem issues.

2. Fear of Judgment

In high society, public image and reputation are invaluable. The fear of judgment or criticism can drive individuals to hide their vulnerabilities, ultimately exacerbating feelings of stress and anxiety. The constant need to project an image of success can be emotionally taxing.

The Loneliness of High Society

Surrounded by wealth and luxury, one might think that loneliness is far from the minds of high-class individuals. However, the reality often contradicts this assumption.

1. Superficial Relationships

High society can be rife with superficial relationships. Many high-class individuals find it challenging to establish genuine connections as they often question others' motivations and intentions. This sense of isolation can lead to feelings of loneliness and despondency.

2. Lack of Privacy

Privacy is a scarce commodity in high society. The constant public scrutiny can make individuals feel exposed and vulnerable, leading to a sense of isolation. It becomes increasingly challenging to find a trusted confidant or a safe space to discuss personal issues.

The Weight of Social Expectations

The demands and expectations of high society can place an immense burden on individuals. The fear of not living up to these expectations can lead to stress and anxiety.

1. Social Obligations

High-class individuals often have a calendar filled with social obligations. Whether it's attending fundraisers, charity events, or galas, the pressure to be present and engage with others can be overwhelming. The fear of disappointing others or being seen as unsocial can create a constant source of stress.

2. Competitive Nature

High society is highly competitive. The pursuit of status, recognition, and success can lead to a never-ending race. The constant comparison with peers can erode self-worth and contribute to anxiety. The fear of falling behind can be paralyzing.

The Emotional Toll of Maintaining Appearances

The facade of perfection is emotionally taxing. High-class individuals often suppress their emotions to maintain a polished image.

1. Emotional Suppression

The need to uphold an image of success can lead to the suppression of genuine emotions. Individuals may hide their fears, insecurities, and vulnerabilities, causing emotional turmoil. This emotional suppression can lead to a host of mental health issues, including anxiety and depression.

2. Lack of Authenticity

The pressure to maintain appearances can stifle authenticity. High-class individuals may feel compelled to conform to societal norms and expectations, resulting in a lack of self-expression. This can contribute to feelings of dissatisfaction and emptiness.

Coping Mechanisms in High Society

Despite the challenges, high-class individuals often employ various coping mechanisms to deal with their mental health struggles.

1. Therapy and Counseling

Many high-class individuals seek therapy and counseling to cope with the demands of their lifestyle. Therapists offer a safe space for discussing anxieties and fears, providing valuable support and guidance.

2. Retreats and Wellness Getaways

Wellness retreats and getaways are popular among high-class individuals seeking respite from their hectic lives. These retreats provide a break from the constant pressure to maintain appearances and offer tools for stress management.

3. Mindfulness and Meditation

Practicing mindfulness and meditation can help high-class individuals manage stress and anxiety. These techniques promote self-awareness and emotional regulation, allowing them to better navigate their mental health struggles.

The Importance of Support Networks

Support networks play a crucial role in helping high-class individuals manage their mental health issues.

1. Family and Friends

Having a strong support system of family and friends who understand the unique challenges of high society can be invaluable. These trusted individuals offer a safe space for vulnerability and support in times of need.

2. Professional Guidance

Mental health professionals, including therapists and counselors, offer guidance and strategies for managing stress, anxiety, and the pressure to maintain appearances. Seeking professional help is an essential step in addressing mental health issues effectively.

Destigmatizing Mental Health in High Society

To address mental health struggles in high society, it's essential to break down the stigma associated with seeking help.

1. Public Advocacy

Prominent figures in high society can use their influence to advocate for mental health awareness. By sharing their own experiences and supporting mental health initiatives, they can help destigmatize seeking help.

2. Education and Awareness

Educating high-class individuals about mental health and the common struggles they face is crucial. Greater awareness can lead to more individuals seeking help and support when needed.

Conclusion

The world of high society is not the utopian paradise it may seem to be. High-class individuals face their own set of unique challenges, including the pressure to maintain appearances, unrealistic expectations, and the emotional toll of their lifestyle. Stress, anxiety, and loneliness often lurk behind the glamorous facade, making it essential to address the mental health struggles within this social stratum.

Navigating these challenges involves seeking support from trusted networks, mental health professionals, and employing coping mechanisms such as therapy, mindfulness, and wellness retreats. Ultimately, the destigmatization of mental health issues in high society is critical to ensuring that those living in this world can lead happier, healthier lives. As high-class individuals become more open about their experiences, they can pave the way for a more empathetic and understanding society, where mental health is a priority for all, regardless of social standing.

Chapter 7. Unrealistic Expectations and Perfectionism

Introduction

High society, a world of opulence and privilege, is often romanticized in the media and the collective imagination. Yet, beneath the glitz and glamour, this social stratum is not immune to its own set of challenges and pitfalls. One of the most pervasive issues is the burden of unrealistic expectations and perfectionism that many high-class individuals grapple with. In this article, we delve into the world of the elite and explore how these unrealistic expectations and the unrelenting pursuit of perfection can lead to constant dissatisfaction and stress.

The Allure of High Society

High society has always captivated people's imaginations. The elegant galas, exquisite fashion, and luxurious lifestyles on display in glossy magazines and social media feeds can make anyone long for a taste of this extravagant world. However, as alluring as it may seem from the outside, high society comes with its own set of challenges.

The Pressure to Conform

The high-class society often exerts tremendous pressure on individuals to conform to certain standards. This pressure stems from a variety of sources.

Social Circles: Members of high society tend to move within tight-knit social circles, where certain behaviors, appearances, and values are expected. Deviating from these norms can lead to social ostracism.

Public Image: Maintaining a flawless public image is paramount in high society. The fear of reputational damage and scrutiny can be paralyzing, pushing individuals to mask their vulnerabilities and struggles.

Unrealistic Beauty Standards

In the world of high society, the pursuit of physical perfection is relentless. The fixation on appearance often leads to:

Invasive Cosmetic Procedures: Many individuals resort to extensive cosmetic surgeries and procedures to attain an idealized version of beauty. The quest for the "perfect" face and body can become an obsession.

Body Image Issues: The constant comparison with others can lead to body image issues and eating disorders, as individuals strive to fit into unrealistic beauty standards.

The Strain of Wealth

While immense wealth can provide a comfortable and luxurious life, it also brings its own set of challenges.

Materialism: High society often emphasizes material possessions as a measure of success. The pressure to acquire extravagant homes, cars, and designer wardrobes can lead to excessive consumerism and financial stress.

Fear of Losing Status: Wealthy individuals frequently fear losing their financial standing. This fear can push them to work excessively and prioritize their wealth over their well-being.

Perfectionism and Its Consequences

Perfectionism is a common trait in high society. The relentless pursuit of excellence can have several detrimental consequences.

Constant Stress: The quest for perfection leads to unrelenting stress. Individuals are driven by an unattainable standard that keeps them in a perpetual state of anxiety.

Fear of Failure: Perfectionists dread failure, often avoiding taking risks or trying new things. This fear can hinder personal growth and creativity.

The Impact on Mental Health

The unrealistic expectations and perfectionism that pervade high society can significantly impact mental health.

Anxiety and Depression: Many high-class individuals struggle with anxiety and depression as they battle to meet lofty standards and navigate the constant pressure to perform.

Loneliness and Isolation: Despite being surrounded by a social circle, high society can be an incredibly lonely place. The fear of vulnerability and judgment can lead to a sense of isolation.

Navigating Unrealistic Expectations

For those in high society, it is essential to navigate these unrealistic expectations and perfectionism effectively.

Self-Compassion: Learning to be kind to oneself and accepting imperfections can help combat perfectionism and reduce stress.

Seek Professional Help: Therapists and counselors can provide valuable support in addressing mental health concerns related to unrealistic expectations.

Reevaluate Values: High society individuals should reflect on their values and determine whether they align with the societal norms they've been pressured to adopt.

The Role of Support Systems

Support systems are crucial in helping high-class individuals combat unrealistic expectations and perfectionism.

Friends and Family: A strong support network can offer emotional support and provide a safe space for individuals to express their vulnerabilities.

Building Authentic Relationships: Encouraging authentic and genuine connections can help alleviate the isolation experienced by high society members.

Changing the Culture

To address the issue of unrealistic expectations and perfectionism in high society, a broader cultural shift is necessary.

Redefine Success: High society should move away from purely materialistic definitions of success and embrace a broader, more holistic perspective.

Promote Diversity: Encouraging diversity and celebrating individuality can reduce the pressure to conform to narrow standards.

Conclusion

High society, with its allure and privilege, may seem like a dream come true, but beneath the surface, unrealistic expectations and perfectionism cast a long shadow. The pressure to conform to societal norms, maintain a perfect image, and amass wealth can lead to constant dissatisfaction and stress.

As high society individuals grapple with these challenges, it is crucial to reevaluate their values, seek support from friends and family, and work towards a cultural shift that promotes diversity and a broader definition of success. In doing so, they can free themselves from the suffocating grasp of unrealistic expectations and perfectionism, leading to a more fulfilling and authentic life.

Introduction

In the world of high society, where opulence and privilege reign, the dynamics of family relationships take on a unique and complex dimension. High-class families often find themselves juggling the demands of busy schedules, societal expectations, and a lifestyle that can be both a blessing and a curse. In this article, we will delve into the intricacies of family dynamics and relationships within high-class circles. We'll explore the challenges these families encounter, as well as strategies to maintain healthy, fulfilling relationships in the face of constant scrutiny and high expectations.

The Pressures of High Society

High-class families operate in an environment where the spotlight is always shining. The expectations of maintaining a certain image and reputation are incredibly high. From glamorous galas to philanthropic endeavors, they are expected to be involved in a wide array of social events. However, these societal pressures can strain family dynamics.

One of the most significant challenges is the constant scrutiny and gossip that surrounds high-class families. Every move, decision, and relationship is subject to public opinion, which can create an atmosphere of anxiety and self-consciousness.

To navigate these pressures successfully, high-class families must establish a strong support system within their family unit. Open communication, trust, and a united front are essential in facing external pressures while keeping the family's well-being intact.

Managing Busy Schedules

High-class families often have incredibly busy schedules. High-profile careers, charity events, and social commitments can make it challenging to find quality time for family. The constant hustle and bustle can strain relationships as family members struggle to find common ground.

To overcome this challenge, families must prioritize quality over quantity when it comes to spending time together. They can create traditions and routines that allow them to bond, even in the midst of hectic lives. Whether it's a weekly family dinner or a monthly getaway, setting aside dedicated family time is crucial.

The Impact on Children

Children growing up in high-class families face their own set of challenges. They often find themselves in the limelight from a young age, leading to immense pressure to meet societal expectations. The expectations to excel academically, socially, and professionally can be overwhelming.

To nurture healthy relationships within the family, parents should strive to shield their children from the harsher aspects of public life. This can include limiting exposure to the media and prioritizing their emotional well-being. Quality time with children is especially important, as it provides a safe space for them to share their thoughts and feelings without fear of judgment.

Spousal Relationships

Marital relationships in high-class families can be particularly challenging to maintain. The demands of public life, busy schedules, and external pressures can strain even the most loving partnerships. Maintaining a healthy spousal relationship is vital for the overall well-being of the family.

Couples in high society should prioritize their relationship by setting aside private time, focusing on effective communication, and seeking support when needed. Marriage counseling or therapy can be a valuable resource to help couples navigate the unique challenges they face.

Generational Differences

High-class families often span multiple generations, each with its own values, expectations, and experiences. These generational differences can lead to conflicts and misunderstandings within the family.

To bridge these gaps, open communication is essential. Creating an environment where family members from different generations can express their viewpoints without judgment is crucial. This allows for the exchange of wisdom and experiences that can enrich the family's overall dynamics.

Maintaining Privacy

The need for privacy is often at odds with the high visibility that comes with high society. Maintaining a sense of privacy is challenging, and families often find themselves walking a fine line between sharing their lives with the public and safeguarding their personal space.

It's important for high-class families to establish boundaries that protect their privacy while allowing them to fulfill their public roles. These boundaries should be communicated clearly to family members and respected by those in their social and professional circles.

Dealing with Scandals

Scandals and controversies are almost inevitable in high society. The fallout from such events can take a toll on family relationships, leading to mistrust, blame, and emotional distress.

To navigate scandals successfully, high-class families must address the issue as a united front. Open discussions and problem-solving can help the family move past the incident and emerge stronger. Seeking professional guidance, such as legal or public relations support, can also be valuable in managing the fallout.

Mental Health and Coping Mechanisms

The stress and pressure of high society can take a significant toll on family members' mental health. It's essential for families to recognize the signs of stress and prioritize their well-being.

Encouraging open conversations about mental health, providing access to professional support, and promoting healthy coping mechanisms can help family members manage the unique stressors they face. Practicing self-care and stress reduction techniques can be instrumental in maintaining emotional balance.

Involving Extended Family

High-class families often have extensive networks of extended family members. These relationships can add depth and support to the family dynamic, but they can also introduce additional complexities and expectations.

Involving extended family members should be done thoughtfully, with clear communication about boundaries and expectations. While extended family can provide valuable support, it's essential to ensure that their involvement doesn't create undue pressure or conflicts within the family.

The Role of Family Advisors

Many high-class families employ family advisors to help them navigate the intricacies of their social and financial responsibilities. These advisors play a vital role in maintaining the family's well-being and cohesion.

Selecting trustworthy and experienced family advisors is essential. These individuals can provide guidance on financial matters, family governance, and conflict resolution, helping to create a stable and harmonious family environment.

Conclusion

High-class families face a myriad of challenges in maintaining healthy relationships amidst their busy schedules and high societal expectations. To thrive in this unique environment, they must prioritize open communication, quality time, and support networks within their family unit. Additionally, the careful management of privacy, boundaries, and external pressures is essential for preserving their relationships. By addressing these challenges head-on, high-class families can foster strong, resilient, and harmonious family dynamics that withstand the pressures of high society.

Introduction

In today's fast-paced world, many individuals find themselves grappling with the delicate juggling act of balancing demanding careers and personal lives. High society, often associated with prestige, success, and the pursuit of excellence, presents unique challenges in achieving this balance. In this article, we will explore the intricacies of work-life imbalance in high society and provide practical strategies for attaining a more harmonious and fulfilling lifestyle. By addressing the difficulties of this delicate equilibrium, we aim to offer valuable insights for those navigating the challenges of a high-society lifestyle.

The High Society Dilemma

1. The All-Consuming Career

High society often demands relentless dedication to one's career. In competitive fields such as finance, law, and entertainment, the pressure to excel can lead to excessive work hours, frequent business trips, and constant connectivity. This all-encompassing commitment can strain personal relationships and diminish the quality of life outside of work.

To address this dilemma:

Set Boundaries: Establish clear boundaries between work and personal life. Define working hours, and make a conscious effort to disconnect from work-related responsibilities when your workday ends.

Prioritize Self-Care: Recognize the importance of self-care and relaxation. Allocate time for activities that rejuvenate your mind and body, whether it's yoga, meditation, or simply a leisurely walk in the park.

2. Social Obligations

High society often comes with a barrage of social engagements, from galas and fundraisers to networking events and charity functions. While these events can be enriching, they can also be overwhelming and time-consuming, leaving little room for personal life.

To find a balance:

Selective Participation: Be selective about the social events you attend. Prioritize those that truly matter to you and align with your personal values. It's perfectly acceptable to decline some invitations in favor of quality personal time.

Delegate Responsibilities: If possible, delegate your responsibilities at these events. This can free up your time and reduce the stress associated with juggling social obligations with personal life.

3. Family and Relationship Strain

The demands of high society can place considerable strain on family and personal relationships. Spouses, children, and close friends often bear the brunt of your career's demands, leading to emotional distance and dissatisfaction.

To nurture relationships:

Effective Communication: Open, honest communication is crucial. Discuss your work-related commitments and schedule with your loved ones, and involve them in decision-making processes that may impact your personal life.

Quality Over Quantity: Make the most of the time you spend with loved ones. Quality interactions are more valuable than sheer quantity. Plan memorable activities and create cherished moments together.

Strategies for a Balanced Lifestyle in High Society

1. Time Management

Effective time management is a cornerstone of achieving work-life balance, especially in high society. By optimizing your use of time, you can maintain a successful career while still enjoying a fulfilling personal life.

Prioritization: Identify your most important tasks and allocate time to them. The Eisenhower Matrix, which categorizes tasks as urgent and important, can help you focus on what truly matters.

Time Blocking: Allocate specific time blocks for work, personal life, and self-care. Stick to this schedule as closely as possible to ensure a balanced life.

Outsourcing: Delegate tasks that can be handled by others, such as administrative work or household chores. Outsourcing can free up valuable time.

2. Embrace Technology Mindfully

While technology has revolutionized our lives, it can also contribute to work-life imbalance when used indiscriminately. High-society individuals often have the latest gadgets and apps at their disposal, which can blur the line between work and personal life.

Digital Detox: Schedule regular digital detox periods during the day. Turn off notifications and limit screen time to create space for personal connections and relaxation.

Use Technology Wisely: Leverage technology to streamline tasks and improve efficiency, but be mindful of its impact on your personal life. Seek a balance between the convenience of technology and the need for unplugged moments.

3. Delegate and Seek Support

In high society, there's often a perception that success requires complete self-sufficiency. However, seeking support and delegating tasks can be essential for maintaining work-life balance.

Delegate at Work: If possible, delegate tasks at your workplace. Recognize that you don't have to do everything yourself and that others can contribute to the team's success.

Household Assistance: Consider hiring household help to manage daily chores. This can free up your time for more meaningful activities.

4. Practice Mindfulness

Mindfulness is the practice of being fully present in the moment, which can significantly improve work-life balance. By cultivating mindfulness, high-society individuals can reduce stress, improve focus, and enhance their personal lives.

Mindful Breathing: Engage in deep, conscious breathing exercises throughout the day to calm your mind and reduce stress.

Meditation: Establish a regular meditation practice to promote emotional well-being and reduce the mental clutter that can interfere with work-life balance.

5. Personal Wellness

Taking care of your physical and mental health is paramount in high society. Neglecting your well-being can lead to burnout and hinder your ability to balance work and personal life.

Regular Exercise: Make time for physical activity to maintain your health and reduce stress. Regular exercise can boost your energy levels and improve overall well-being.

Healthy Eating: A balanced diet is essential. Avoid excessive consumption of caffeine and alcohol, as they can disrupt your sleep patterns and affect your ability to unwind.

6. Set Realistic Goals

In the pursuit of success in high society, individuals often set ambitious goals that leave little room for personal life. Setting more realistic and balanced goals is essential for work-life equilibrium.

SMART Goals: Utilize the SMART (Specific, Measurable, Achievable, Relevant, and Time-bound) framework for goal setting. This approach encourages you to set attainable objectives that consider personal life.

Regular Review: Periodically review your goals and make necessary adjustments. Ensure that your objectives align with your values and personal life priorities.

7. Learn to Say No

The ability to say no is a powerful tool in achieving work-life balance. In high society, there is often pressure to say yes to every opportunity, but this can lead to overcommitment and burnout.

Polite Declination: When declining an invitation or request, do so politely and respectfully. You don't have to provide a lengthy explanation, but express your gratitude for the opportunity.

Effective Time Management: By saying no strategically, you can allocate more time and energy to the activities that matter most to you, both professionally and personally.

8. Seek Professional Help

If work-life imbalance is causing significant distress or impacting your mental health, don't hesitate to seek professional assistance. A therapist or counselor can provide guidance and strategies to help you regain balance.

Conclusion

Work-life balance is a challenging endeavor for individuals in high society, where demanding careers and social obligations often take precedence. By employing these strategies, you can achieve a more harmonious and fulfilling lifestyle. Remember that the journey to balance is ongoing, and it's essential to adapt these strategies to your unique circumstances. Embrace the idea that a balanced life is not only achievable but crucial for long-term success and happiness in high society.

Introduction

High-class individuals, often synonymous with wealth and privilege, find themselves navigating a unique set of ethical dilemmas. While they possess resources and influence that can significantly impact society, they also grapple with profound questions of responsibility, accountability, and moral choices. In this article, we delve into the ethical considerations that confront high-class individuals, including philanthropy, responsible business practices, and societal contributions. These individuals are often seen as role models, and the decisions they make can ripple across society. Hence, it is imperative to explore these dilemmas within the context of high society.

Philanthropy: A Double-Edged Sword

Philanthropy is a hallmark of high-class individuals, with vast fortunes at their disposal. However, it presents a double-edged sword, raising significant ethical dilemmas.

Impact vs. Intent: Many high-class individuals engage in philanthropy, seeking to make a positive impact on society. However, questions arise regarding their intent. Are they genuinely committed to social change, or is it a mere public relations exercise to enhance their image?

Unequal Distribution: The scale of their philanthropic endeavors often overshadows government efforts, raising concerns about the concentration of power in the hands of a few. Does philanthropy perpetuate social inequality, allowing the wealthy to dictate social priorities?

Accountability and Transparency: High-class individuals must grapple with questions of accountability and transparency in their philanthropic endeavors. Do they owe it to society to be more transparent about their giving, and how do they ensure their donations are used for the intended purposes?

Influence Over Policy: Their financial clout can also translate into influence over policy decisions. This raises concerns about the ethical boundary between philanthropy and political manipulation. To what extent should high-class individuals be allowed to shape public policy through their giving?

Responsible Business Practices: A Moral Imperative

High-class individuals often wield considerable power as business leaders. Responsible business practices are essential, and ethical dilemmas emerge in this domain.

Corporate Social Responsibility (CSR): Many high-class individuals lead or own major corporations, making CSR a significant concern. How can they balance profitability with ethical obligations to employees, customers, and the environment?

Exploitation vs. Empowerment: The power dynamics within corporations can lead to ethical dilemmas. Do high-class individuals prioritize profit at the expense of fair treatment, or do they genuinely seek to empower their workforce?

Environmental Sustainability: As stewards of the environment, high-class individuals face critical ethical decisions related to sustainability. Should they invest in eco-friendly practices, even if it means sacrificing short-term profits?

Taxation and Fair Play: High-class individuals also face scrutiny for their role in shaping taxation policies. Are they engaged in tax avoidance practices, contributing to the growing wealth gap, or are they advocates for fair and equitable tax systems?

Societal Contributions: Balancing Privilege and Responsibility

Society looks up to high-class individuals as leaders and role models. Their actions have the power to inspire and uplift communities, but this comes with its own set of ethical dilemmas.

Cultural Appropriation: In the pursuit of societal contributions, high-class individuals may inadvertently engage in cultural appropriation. *Cultural appropriation* refers to the adoption or use of elements from one culture by individuals or groups from a different culture, often without understanding or respecting the cultural significance and context, which can be considered disrespectful or harmful. How can they engage with different cultures respectfully and ethically?

Public Image vs. Authenticity: The high society often demands a carefully curated public image. How can high-class individuals balance their authentic selves with the societal expectations placed upon them?

Advocacy and Activism: Many choose to use their platform for advocacy and activism, but the line between raising awareness and virtue signaling can be thin. *Virtue signaling* is the act of publicly expressing one's moral or political values or beliefs, often on social media, to gain approval or demonstrate one's righteousness, sometimes without genuine commitment to action or change. What are the ethical considerations in leveraging their influence for social change?

Gentrification: Their investments in communities can lead to gentrification, displacing local residents. *Gentrification* is the process by which wealthier individuals or groups move into a previously lower-income or working-class neighborhood, often leading to rising property values, rent prices, and cultural changes, which can displace long-term residents and businesses. How can high-class individuals contribute to the betterment of a neighborhood without contributing to its social fragmentation?

Case Studies: Navigating Ethical Dilemmas

Examining real-life case studies provides insight into how high-class individuals navigate these ethical dilemmas.

The Gates Foundation: The Gates Foundation's philanthropic endeavors have transformed public health and education, but concerns about their influence on global health policy have been raised.

Patagonia's Environmental Advocacy: The outdoor clothing company Patagonia is a prime example of a corporation prioritizing environmental sustainability, but their business practices are not without controversy.

Elon Musk: As a prominent figure in both business and technology, Musk's ethical decisions, from electric vehicles to space exploration, have stirred debates on responsible innovation and wealth distribution.

Angelina Jolie's Humanitarian Work: The actress and humanitarian has leveraged her fame for good, but her approach to international adoption and issues of cultural appropriation have sparked discussions.

Conclusion

High-class individuals face a myriad of ethical dilemmas stemming from their wealth, power, and privilege. Whether through philanthropy, responsible business practices, or societal contributions, their decisions have far-reaching consequences. In navigating these dilemmas, high-class individuals must find a balance between their personal aspirations and their ethical responsibilities to society. Acknowledging the complexity of these issues is the first step in fostering ethical decision-making and positive change within high society. Only by addressing these dilemmas with integrity and a genuine commitment to the betterment of society can high-class individuals truly become role models and leaders in the ethical evolution of our world.

Introduction

Success has long been associated with material wealth, power, and recognition in our society. The pursuit of these traditional markers of success has often led to a neglect of holistic well-being, personal growth, and meaningful connections. In the realm of high society, these pressures can be even more pronounced. This article seeks to challenge conventional notions of success and propose alternative definitions that emphasize a more balanced and fulfilling approach to life. We will explore the importance of holistic well-being, personal growth, and meaningful connections as pillars of a new definition of success.

The Conventional Notion of Success

The traditional definition of success is typically centered around the accumulation of wealth, power, and status. High society often amplifies these expectations, with individuals feeling the need to constantly outdo one another in the pursuit of material achievements. While these achievements can bring temporary satisfaction, they often come at a high cost, with individuals sacrificing their well-being and personal growth for the sake of success.

Holistic Well-Being

1. Physical Health

A redefined version of success places a strong emphasis on holistic well-being, starting with physical health. High society often involves hectic schedules and demanding work commitments that can lead to neglecting one's physical health. Success should not come at the cost of physical well-being. It's essential to prioritize regular exercise, a balanced diet, and adequate sleep to maintain good health.

2. Mental Health

Mental health is another vital component of holistic well-being. High-achievers in high society are not immune to stress, anxiety, and burnout. A new definition of success should include emotional and mental well-being as a core element. Practices like meditation, mindfulness, and seeking professional help when needed should be encouraged.

3. Work-Life Balance

Balancing work and personal life is crucial for overall well-being. A successful life should involve quality time with family and friends, pursuing hobbies, and taking regular breaks to recharge. High society often pushes individuals to work incessantly, but a redefined success acknowledges the value of work-life balance.

Personal Growth

1. Continuous Learning

Personal growth should be a central element of success. This involves a commitment to lifelong learning and self-improvement. High society can sometimes foster complacency, as individuals reach a certain level of financial success. A redefined success encourages individuals to continue learning, exploring new skills, and seeking personal development.

2. Purpose and Passion

Success should be linked to finding purpose and passion in life. High society often prioritizes financial gains over personal fulfillment. A new definition of success values the pursuit of one's passions and aligning them with a sense of purpose. This not only leads to personal satisfaction but also contributes positively to society.

3. Resilience

Personal growth includes building resilience. High society can be a place of constant scrutiny and competition. Success, in this context, should involve the ability to bounce back from failures and setbacks. Resilience is a valuable skill that helps individuals navigate the challenges of high society.

Meaningful Connections

1. Authentic Relationships

In a redefined version of success, meaningful connections take precedence over superficial interactions. High society can sometimes promote networking solely for personal gain. True success should involve nurturing authentic relationships based on trust, respect, and mutual support. These connections provide emotional sustenance and often lead to opportunities beyond one's material wealth.

2. Giving Back

Success should also entail giving back to society. High society often hoards its wealth, but a new definition of success emphasizes philanthropy and supporting social causes. By making a positive impact on the lives of others, individuals can find deeper fulfillment and meaning in their own success.

3. Family and Community

Meaningful connections extend to family and community. In the pursuit of traditional success, it's easy to neglect these vital bonds. A redefined version of success recognizes the importance of family and community involvement. These connections provide a strong support system and a sense of belonging.

Overcoming Challenges

Challenging the traditional definition of success is not without its difficulties, especially in high society, where societal pressures and expectations can be overwhelming. However, redefining success can lead to a more balanced and fulfilling life.

1. Resistance from the Status Quo

Changing one's approach to success may face resistance from the established norms of high society. The pressure to conform to traditional success standards can be intense, but it's essential to stay true to your values and priorities.

2. Redefining Success for Future Generations

Redefining success can have a profound impact on future generations. High society often sets the example for what is considered successful. By promoting a new definition that prioritizes well-being, personal growth, and meaningful connections, you can inspire positive change in society.

Practical Steps for Redefined Success

To implement this alternative definition of success, consider the following practical steps:

1. Self-Reflection

Begin by reflecting on your values and what truly matters to you. What does success mean to you personally? Align your goals with your values.

2. Set Balanced Goals

Set goals that encompass not only financial and professional achievements but also personal growth, well-being, and meaningful connections.

3. Create a Supportive Environment

Surround yourself with people who share your values and encourage your pursuit of a redefined success. A supportive network can make a significant difference.

4. Practice Gratitude

Regularly practice gratitude to appreciate the meaningful aspects of your life. This can help you stay focused on what truly matters.

5. Seek Professional Guidance

If you're struggling to break free from traditional definitions of success, consider seeking the guidance of a therapist or life coach who can help you realign your priorities.

Conclusion

Redefining success in high society is a necessary and transformative endeavor. It challenges the narrow, materialistic view of success and elevates the importance of holistic well-being, personal growth, and meaningful connections. By pursuing this alternative definition, individuals can lead more balanced, fulfilling lives, and inspire positive change in society. Success should be measured not by the size of your bank account or the number of titles you hold, but by the depth of your well-being, the extent of your personal growth, and the richness of your meaningful connections.

Introduction

In the whirlwind of high society, where glittering galas, social obligations, and high-pressure demands abound, it's easy to get caught up in a whirlwind of stress and anxiety. The high-class individuals who inhabit this rarefied world may enjoy privileges, but they are not immune to the toll that relentless schedules and expectations can take on their well-being. In this article, we explore the importance of mindfulness and well-being strategies in helping high-class individuals manage stress and find contentment.

Understanding the High-Class Lifestyle

Before diving into mindfulness practices and well-being strategies, it's crucial to understand the unique challenges that high-class individuals face. While the perks of wealth and privilege are undeniable, they often come with a set of stressors that can be quite different from those faced by the average person.

1. Constant Public Scrutiny

High-class individuals often live under the relentless scrutiny of the public eye. Every move they make, every word they utter is analyzed, criticized, or praised. This constant attention can lead to immense pressure and stress, as they feel the need to maintain a certain image and reputation.

2. Demanding Social Obligations

High society often comes with a plethora of social obligations, including attending numerous events, galas, and parties. While these occasions can be enjoyable, the frequency and expectations associated with them can be overwhelming, leaving little room for personal time and relaxation.

3. High-Pressure Decision Making

Whether it's running a business empire or managing a vast investment portfolio, high-class individuals often have to make high-stakes decisions. The weight of these decisions can take a toll on their mental health, leading to anxiety and stress.

4. Isolation and Loneliness

Surprisingly, amidst all the glitz and glamour, high-class individuals may find themselves feeling isolated and lonely. Building genuine connections can be difficult when surrounded by people who often have their own agendas.

The Role of Mindfulness in High Society

Mindfulness, a practice rooted in ancient traditions like Buddhism, has become a powerful tool for managing stress, anxiety, and finding contentment. High-class individuals can benefit immensely from incorporating mindfulness into their lives.

1. Stress Reduction

Mindfulness techniques, such as meditation and deep breathing, help high-class individuals manage stress by allowing them to take a step back from their demanding lives and find moments of peace. These practices enable them to stay focused, calm, and collected in the face of challenging situations.

2. Increased Resilience

The practice of mindfulness builds emotional resilience. High-class individuals can learn to bounce back from setbacks more effectively and face adversity with a greater sense of composure.

3. Enhanced Decision Making

Mindfulness cultivates clarity of thought and improved decision-making abilities. High-class individuals can use mindfulness to gain a fresh perspective on complex issues, ultimately leading to more informed choices.

4. Improved Emotional Regulation

With mindfulness, high-class individuals can better regulate their emotions, reducing the risk of impulsivity and emotional outbursts. This is crucial when faced with high-pressure situations and decisions.

Practical Mindfulness Techniques

Now that we've highlighted the benefits of mindfulness, let's delve into some practical techniques that high-class individuals can incorporate into their busy lives.

1. Meditation

Regular meditation practice can be a game-changer for high-class individuals. Allocating as little as 10-15 minutes each day for meditation can significantly reduce stress and enhance mental clarity.

2. Mindful Breathing

Mindful breathing is a technique that can be done anywhere, even during a hectic gala or a business meeting. It involves taking a moment to focus on your breath, which helps ground you and reduce stress.

3. Mindful Eating

In high society, dining is often a social event. Practicing mindful eating involves savoring each bite, paying attention to the flavors and textures of the food, and enjoying the experience fully. This can transform mealtime into a calming, mindful ritual.

4. Digital Detox

High-class individuals are often tethered to their smartphones and devices. A digital detox, even for short periods, can provide a much-needed break from constant connectivity and help clear the mind.

Prioritizing Well-being in High Society

Well-being encompasses physical, mental, and emotional health. While mindfulness plays a crucial role, there are other well-being strategies that high-class individuals should consider.

1. Regular Exercise

Exercise is a well-known stress reliever and mood enhancer. High-class individuals should make time for regular physical activity, whether it's in the form of yoga, jogging, or hitting the gym.

2. Adequate Sleep

Sleep is essential for maintaining well-being. High-class individuals must prioritize quality sleep to ensure they are well-rested and can face their busy schedules with vitality.

3. Nutrition and Hydration

A balanced diet rich in nutrients and staying well-hydrated is vital for physical and mental health. Proper nutrition can enhance energy levels and cognitive functioning.

4. Seeking Professional Support

High-class individuals should not hesitate to seek professional support when needed. Therapy or counseling can provide valuable insights and strategies for managing stress and improving overall well-being.

Balancing Social Obligations and Personal Time

High-class individuals often struggle to find personal time amidst a whirlwind of social obligations. It's essential to strike a balance that allows them to maintain their well-being.

1. Set Boundaries

Learning to say no and setting boundaries is crucial. High-class individuals should not overcommit to social events and be selective about the ones they attend.

2. Prioritize Self-Care

Make self-care a non-negotiable part of the schedule. This can include activities like spa treatments, quiet evenings at home, or a weekend getaway to rejuvenate.

3. Quality Over Quantity

Focus on the quality of social interactions rather than the quantity. Building deep, meaningful relationships with a few individuals can be more fulfilling than trying to maintain a large social circle.

The Importance of Connection

While high society often brings isolation and loneliness, building genuine connections is paramount for well-being.

1. Authentic Relationships

Seek out authentic relationships that go beyond social obligations. Building connections based on shared interests and values can provide a deep sense of fulfillment.

2. Supportive Communities

High-class individuals should explore or create supportive communities where they can connect with like-minded people. This can provide a sense of belonging and emotional support.

3. Volunteering and Philanthropy

Engaging in charitable work or philanthropy can create a sense of purpose and connection. High-class individuals can use their resources to make a positive impact in society, fostering a sense of fulfillment.

The Power of Gratitude

In the fast-paced world of high society, it's easy to lose sight of the many blessings one has. Practicing gratitude can be a simple yet effective way to find contentment.

1. Gratitude Journal

High-class individuals can maintain a gratitude journal, jotting down the things they're grateful for each day. This practice can help shift the focus from what's lacking to what's abundant in their lives.

2. Expressing Appreciation

Expressing gratitude to others can strengthen relationships and create a positive, supportive network. A simple thank-you note or gesture of appreciation can go a long way.

3. Mindful Reflection

Take time to reflect mindfully on the privileges and opportunities that come with high-class status. Recognize the advantages and use them to foster a sense of contentment and purpose.

Finding Balance and Contentment

In conclusion, high-class individuals navigating the challenges of high society can promote mindfulness and well-being by incorporating practical techniques into their daily lives. Mindfulness, combined with well-being strategies and a focus on building genuine connections, can help manage stress and find contentment in the midst of a demanding lifestyle.

By prioritizing self-care, setting boundaries, and practicing gratitude, high-class individuals can not only thrive in their social circles but also lead fulfilling, balanced lives. Remember, the pursuit of well-being is not a luxury; it's a necessity for everyone, regardless of their social status. In the dazzling world of high society, finding contentment is the true mark of success.

Chapter 13. Fostering Genuine Relationships

Introduction

In a world where social connections are increasingly fleeting and superficial, the value of fostering genuine relationships cannot be overstated. High society, in particular, presents unique challenges when it comes to building and maintaining authentic connections. The glittering facade of this social landscape often masks a web of superficiality, but beneath the surface, the desire for meaningful relationships persists. In this article, we will explore the art of cultivating authentic connections in high society, providing guidance on how to navigate the challenges that accompany such a social environment.

The Superficiality Trap

High society is often synonymous with glitz, glamour, and a constant stream of social events. However, beneath this veneer lies a peculiar paradox - the prevalence of superficial relationships. Superficiality is, in many ways, a survival strategy in such circles. People keep their guard up, revealing only what they believe will maintain their status and image. This self-preservation mindset can hinder the development of authentic connections.

1. Recognizing the Signs of Superficiality

Surface-level Conversations: Many high society gatherings are filled with small talk, gossip, and discussions about appearances, rather than substantive topics.

Transactional Relationships: Interactions often revolve around networking, favors, and maintaining social hierarchies.

Ephemeral Alliances: Friendships and connections can feel fleeting, as they are often based on convenience rather than genuine interest.

2. The Loneliness Behind the Facade

Amidst all the glitz and glamour, it is not uncommon to find individuals feeling isolated and disconnected. The facade of high society can be isolating, leading many to seek more profound connections.

The Art of Authenticity

Building genuine relationships in high society requires a conscious effort to break free from the superficiality trap and embrace authenticity.

1. Self-Awareness

Understanding Your Values: Before building authentic connections, it's crucial to be clear about your values, beliefs, and what you seek in relationships.

Vulnerability: Being open about your fears, hopes, and insecurities can create a deeper connection with others.

2. Active Listening

Paying Attention: Engage in active listening during conversations, showing genuine interest in what others have to say.

Empathy: **Try to understand the emotions and perspectives of those you're interacting with, fostering a sense of connection.**

3. Be Your True Self

Authenticity: **Don't pretend to be someone you're not to fit in or impress others. Be true to yourself.**

Sharing Your Passions: **Express your genuine interests and hobbies, as they can be a gateway to authentic connections.**

Navigating the High Society Landscape

Building authentic relationships in high society comes with its own set of challenges, but understanding these challenges can help you navigate them more effectively.

1. The Social Hierarchy

Understanding the Power Dynamics: **High society often comes with a clear hierarchy. Be aware of this hierarchy but don't let it dictate your interactions.**

Treating Everyone Equally: **Regardless of status, treat all individuals with respect and kindness.**

2. Handling Superficiality

Steer Conversations Toward Depth: **Be the change you want to see. When engaging in conversations, introduce meaningful topics and encourage others to delve deeper.**

Seek Out Like-Minded Individuals: **Look for those who share your values and interests to build more authentic connections.**

3. Overcoming Judgments

Non-Judgmental Approach: **Approach others without preconceived notions or judgments. Give people a chance to reveal their true selves.**

Resisting Stereotypes: **Avoid categorizing people based on their social status. Remember that everyone has unique experiences and stories.**

Nurturing Authentic Relationships

Building authentic connections is just the beginning. Maintaining these relationships is equally important, and it requires effort and dedication.

1. Consistent Communication

Regular Check-Ins: **Stay in touch with your friends and acquaintances, even if it's just a brief message or call to show you care.**

Meaningful Conversations: **Make time for deeper conversations, sharing experiences and thoughts on life's important matters.**

2. Support and Understanding

Being There in Times of Need: **Offer your support and help when your friends face challenges or difficulties.**

Embrace Differences: **Understand that authentic relationships may involve disagreements, but it's how you handle these differences that matters.**

3. Shared Experiences

Create Memories: **Participate in activities or events together to build shared experiences and strengthen your bond.**

Celebrate Achievements: **Be genuinely happy for your friends' accomplishments and milestones.**

The Power of Authenticity

The rewards of fostering genuine relationships in high society are immeasurable. Authentic connections provide a source of support, trust, and happiness that can significantly enhance your life.

1. Emotional Fulfillment

Reduced Loneliness: **Authentic relationships reduce the isolation often experienced in high society.**

Emotional Support: **Friends who truly understand and care for you can provide valuable emotional support.**

2. Professional Benefits

Networking with Integrity: **Authentic connections can lead to genuine business opportunities and collaborations.**

Trust and Reputation: **Building a reputation for authenticity can enhance your credibility in high society and professional circles.**

3. Improved Well-Being

Reduced Stress: Having a support system of authentic relationships can help reduce stress and anxiety.

Life Satisfaction: Authentic connections can contribute to a higher overall life satisfaction and happiness.

Conclusion

In the world of high society, where superficiality often reigns supreme, the art of fostering genuine relationships is a true testament to one's character. It requires self-awareness, active listening, and the courage to be your true self. While navigating the challenges of this unique social landscape can be daunting, the rewards are worth the effort.

Authentic relationships in high society offer emotional fulfillment, professional benefits, and an overall improved sense of well-being. The key is to break free from the superficiality trap, be mindful of social hierarchies, and embrace authenticity in your interactions.

In the end, what truly matters in high society, as in life, are the meaningful connections we cultivate. By prioritizing genuine relationships, we not only enrich our own lives but also contribute to a more authentic and compassionate high society, creating a positive ripple effect that can extend far beyond the glittering facade.

Introduction

In the realm of high society, where opulence and privilege often reign supreme, it is imperative to discuss the importance of social responsibility and the ways in which individuals of means can give back to society through meaningful contributions. While the high-class lifestyle offers many opportunities for personal enrichment, it also carries a unique set of responsibilities towards the broader community. This article delves into the significance of social responsibility and provides practical suggestions for high-class individuals on how they can engage in philanthropy and make a positive impact on society.

Understanding Social Responsibility

1. The Privilege of High Society

High society is characterized by affluence, privilege, and exclusivity. Those who belong to this stratum often enjoy the finest luxuries life has to offer, from lavish parties and exotic vacations to exquisite art collections and high-end fashion. Yet, with such privilege comes a profound sense of responsibility. High-class individuals are uniquely positioned to make a substantial difference in the lives of others.

2. The Moral Imperative

Social responsibility is a moral imperative for individuals in high society. This responsibility stems from recognizing the disparities and inequalities that exist in the world. Those with the means to do so have a duty to use their resources for the greater good. This responsibility extends beyond one's immediate family or circle to the broader society that has, in one way or another, contributed to their success.

3. Philanthropy as a Core Value

To truly embrace social responsibility, philanthropy must be integrated as a core value within high society. Philanthropy is not merely an option but a fundamental principle that drives positive change. It is about not just giving money but also giving time, expertise, and influence to improve the lives of others and address pressing social issues.

Ways to Give Back

1. Charitable Donations

One of the most straightforward ways for high-class individuals to give back is through charitable donations. Financial contributions to reputable non-profit organizations can support a variety of causes, such as education, healthcare, poverty alleviation, and environmental conservation. It's essential to research and choose organizations that align with your values and objectives.

2. Establishing Foundations and Endowments

Creating a charitable foundation or endowment is another effective way to channel resources into philanthropic endeavors. These structures enable individuals to have greater control over their giving, make a long-term impact, and involve their families in a legacy of social responsibility. Moreover, foundations can provide a tax-efficient way to manage and distribute charitable assets.

3. Impactful Volunteerism

Donating time and expertise can be equally as valuable as financial contributions. High-class individuals can engage in impactful volunteer work by participating in non-profit boards, mentoring underprivileged youth, or providing pro bono services to organizations in need. Their knowledge, skills, and networks can be powerful tools for driving positive change.

Pro bono services are professional services provided by individuals or organizations, such as lawyers, doctors, or consultants, without charging a fee. These services are offered for the public good and typically target individuals or groups who cannot afford to pay for such services. Pro bono work is often done to support a charitable cause, promote access to justice, or address specific social or community needs.

4. Socially Responsible Investing

High society often involves investment portfolios and wealth management strategies. Socially responsible investing (SRI) allows individuals to align their investment decisions with their philanthropic goals. By investing in companies that promote ethical and sustainable practices, they can contribute to positive social and environmental change while generating financial returns.

5. Education and Scholarship Programs

Investing in education is a meaningful way to give back. High-class individuals can establish scholarship programs or fund educational initiatives that provide opportunities to disadvantaged individuals, enabling them to access quality education and pursue their dreams. Education is a transformative force that can break the cycle of poverty and create a more equitable society.

6. Supporting Arts and Culture

The world of high society often has a deep appreciation for the arts and culture. Supporting cultural institutions, museums, and artistic endeavors can be a way to give back. These contributions not only preserve cultural heritage but also enhance the cultural vibrancy of society and promote creativity.

7. Environmental Stewardship

High-class individuals can make a significant impact by focusing on environmental stewardship. Initiatives such as reforestation projects, renewable energy investments, and sustainable agriculture can contribute to a healthier planet. Protecting the environment is not only a responsibility to current generations but to those who will inherit the world in the future.

Challenges in High Society Philanthropy

1. Balancing Personal Goals and Philanthropy

One of the challenges high-class individuals face is striking a balance between personal aspirations and philanthropic endeavors. It can be difficult to allocate time and resources to philanthropy when personal pursuits often demand attention. However, it's crucial to recognize that philanthropy can be personally fulfilling and contribute to long-term happiness and purpose.

2. Avoiding Tokenism

Some may engage in philanthropy for appearances or to gain social status rather than from a genuine desire to make a difference. This tokenistic approach can undermine the true essence of social responsibility. High-class individuals should ensure their philanthropic efforts are sincere and impactful.

3. Building a Sustainable Legacy

Creating a sustainable legacy in philanthropy is a challenge that requires careful planning. High-class individuals should think about how their contributions will continue to make a difference beyond their lifetime. This may involve mentoring the next generation in the family or setting up mechanisms to ensure the perpetuity of their charitable work.

4. Navigating Public Expectations

High-profile individuals in high society often face public scrutiny and high expectations regarding their philanthropic efforts. It can be challenging to meet these expectations while remaining true to one's values and objectives. To overcome this challenge, individuals should be transparent about their philanthropic activities and the causes they support.

While charitable donations can address immediate needs, high-class individuals have the potential to drive systemic change. They can use their influence and connections to advocate for policy changes, promote social justice, and challenge structural inequalities. Achieving lasting impact often requires addressing the root causes of social issues.

Conclusion

Navigating the challenges of high society comes with a distinct responsibility – that of social responsibility. High-class individuals possess the means, influence, and privilege to make a substantial impact on society, and it is their moral imperative to do so. By integrating philanthropy into their lives, they can create a legacy of giving back that enriches not only their own lives but also the lives of countless others.

The ways to give back are diverse, ranging from charitable donations and volunteerism to socially responsible investing and supporting arts and culture. Yet, high-class individuals must also confront challenges in their philanthropic journey, including balancing personal goals, avoiding tokenism, building a sustainable legacy, navigating public expectations, and leveraging influence for systemic change.

Ultimately, embracing social responsibility in high society is a call to action that can lead to a more equitable and compassionate world. By recognizing their unique position and taking meaningful steps to give back, high-class individuals can contribute to a better society, leaving a lasting legacy of positive change for generations to come.

Introduction

Living a high-class lifestyle often conjures images of opulence, luxury, and excess. However, in an age where environmental concerns and sustainability have become paramount, it is imperative that even the high-class community reevaluates their habits and choices. Sustainable living is no longer a buzzword for the eco-conscious; it's a global necessity. This article delves into the significance of adopting environmentally conscious habits within the high-class community, the challenges they face, and the opportunities to promote sustainability.

The High-Class Lifestyle: A Paradigm of Consumption

High society is often associated with extravagance and excess, where status is measured by the size of one's yacht, the rarity of one's wine collection, or the opulence of one's wardrobe. While there's nothing inherently wrong with enjoying the finer things in life, the high-class community's conspicuous consumption has significant environmental consequences.

One of the most glaring issues is the carbon footprint of high-class living. Private jets, luxury cars, and sprawling mansions all come at an environmental cost. The high-class community's disproportionate contribution to carbon emissions cannot be ignored in our efforts to combat climate change. But there is a growing awareness of these issues, and many are beginning to acknowledge the need for change.

Challenges Faced by the High-Class Community

1. Cultural Resistance

One of the primary challenges that the high-class community faces when adopting sustainable lifestyles is cultural resistance. The traditions and habits within high society are deeply ingrained. There's a sense of prestige associated with excessive consumption, and breaking away from these traditions can be met with resistance and even social ostracism.

2. Limited Sustainable Options

Another hurdle is the limited availability of sustainable options within the luxury sector. Sustainable alternatives for high-end products, be it fashion or travel, can be scarce, making it harder for the high-class community to make eco-conscious choices.

3. Social Expectations

High society is often governed by unwritten rules and expectations. These expectations can create immense pressure to maintain a certain standard of living, which often includes wasteful consumption. Deviating from these norms can be socially challenging.

The Significance of Sustainable Lifestyles

High-class individuals have a unique platform and influence that can be harnessed for good. Here's why it's significant for them to adopt sustainable lifestyles:

1. Environmental Impact Reduction

The most apparent reason is to reduce their environmental impact. High-class living typically results in higher carbon footprints, so transitioning to sustainable practices can make a substantial difference.

2. Setting an Example

The high-class community's choices often influence societal trends. By adopting environmentally conscious habits, they can set an example for others to follow, creating a ripple effect towards a more sustainable society.

3. Preserving Natural Resources

Living sustainably helps preserve natural resources. The high-class community often consumes disproportionately, depleting resources that are finite. By making eco-conscious choices, they contribute to the preservation of these resources.

4. Long-Term Viability

Sustainability is not just a buzzword; it's a way to ensure the long-term viability of our planet. High-class individuals, with their resources and reach, can significantly impact the shift towards a more sustainable world.

Promoting Sustainability within High Society

Changing the habits and mindsets of the high-class community is no small feat, but it's entirely possible. Here's how it can be done:

1. Education and Awareness

The first step is to educate the high-class community about the significance of sustainable living. Awareness campaigns, workshops, and seminars can shed light on the environmental consequences of their actions.

2. Providing Sustainable Alternatives

To overcome the challenge of limited sustainable options, the market needs to adapt. Luxury brands can invest in sustainable materials and production methods, offering high-quality, eco-conscious alternatives.

3. Rebranding Sustainability

Sustainability should be seen as a mark of sophistication and class. By rebranding sustainable choices as a symbol of refinement, the high-class community can be encouraged to embrace these practices.

4. Philanthropy and Investment

High-class individuals have substantial resources at their disposal. They can use their wealth and influence for good by supporting eco-friendly initiatives, investing in sustainable businesses, and engaging in philanthropic efforts that promote sustainability.

5. Collaboration with Influencers

Collaborating with influential figures within high society, such as celebrities and business tycoons, can help amplify the message of sustainability. Their endorsements and lifestyle choices can sway public opinion and inspire others to follow suit.

6. Reevaluating Social Norms

Society's expectations and norms within high society need to be reevaluated. The high-class community should feel empowered to redefine what is considered prestigious and admirable. A shift in values is essential to promote sustainable living.

Case Studies of High-Class Sustainability Champions

Several high-class individuals have already embraced sustainable lifestyles and set inspiring examples for their peers. Let's look at a few cases:

1. Prince Harry and Meghan Markle

The Duke and Duchess of Sussex have actively championed environmental causes. They made headlines by choosing to have a small, eco-conscious wedding and advocating for conservation efforts through their charity work.

2. Leonardo DiCaprio

The renowned actor and environmental activist Leonardo DiCaprio is a vocal advocate for climate action. His foundation funds numerous environmental projects and he frequently uses his platform to raise awareness about environmental issues.

3. Stella McCartney

Fashion designer Stella McCartney is a trailblazer in sustainable luxury fashion. Her brand prioritizes eco-friendly materials and ethical practices, demonstrating that high-class fashion can be both stylish and sustainable.

4. Richard Branson

Virgin Group founder Richard Branson is known for his commitment to environmental sustainability. He's invested in renewable energy ventures and advocates for clean energy solutions.

5. Bill and Melinda Gates

The Gates Foundation focuses on global health, poverty alleviation, and, increasingly, climate change. The billionaire philanthropists have pledged significant funds to support innovative sustainability solutions.

Conclusion

In an era marked by climate change and environmental concerns, the high-class community cannot remain oblivious to their role in shaping the planet's future. By adopting environmentally conscious habits and promoting sustainability, they can become catalysts for positive change. This shift not only benefits the environment but also sets a new standard of sophistication and class. Sustainability is not just a lifestyle choice; it's a moral obligation, and the high-class community must lead the way in this transformative journey towards a more sustainable world.

Introduction

Living in high society often comes with its unique set of challenges and demands. The glitz and glamour of this lifestyle can be enticing, but it can also lead to a hectic and unbalanced existence if not managed properly. Achieving a balanced lifestyle is essential, as it allows individuals to flourish in their personal and professional lives. In this article, we will explore practical advice on how to strike that crucial balance between work and personal life, the importance of setting boundaries, and the significance of pursuing passions beyond material pursuits.

The Perils of High Society

High society is a world of opulence, social events, and high-stake networking. People living within these circles often find themselves swept up in the whirlwind of endless gatherings, meetings, and social obligations. While this lifestyle can be rewarding, it can also lead to burnout and a lack of fulfillment if not managed with intention. Let's delve into the challenges faced by individuals in high society and how to address them effectively.

Work-Life Balance: A Prerequisite for Well-being

Achieving work-life balance is a fundamental requirement for everyone, regardless of their social status. For those in high society, the pressure to maintain their status and reputation can often lead to a relentless focus on work, which in turn disrupts the equilibrium between personal life and professional commitments.

1. Prioritize Self-Care

Self-care is the cornerstone of a balanced lifestyle. In high society, it's easy to overlook self-care as a luxury when, in fact, it should be considered a necessity. To prioritize self-care, individuals should allocate time in their schedules for activities that promote relaxation, stress reduction, and overall well-being. This may include exercise, meditation, spending quality time with loved ones, or simply having moments of solitude.

2. Define Clear Boundaries

Setting clear boundaries between work and personal life is essential for maintaining a balanced lifestyle. In high society, it's common for work-related obligations to spill over into personal time. To prevent this, individuals should establish specific boundaries, such as designating certain hours for work and others for leisure. Communicate these boundaries to colleagues and employers to ensure they are respected.

3. Avoid Overcommitment

The allure of high society events and opportunities can lead to overcommitment, leaving individuals feeling overwhelmed. To avoid this, carefully assess each commitment and prioritize those that align with personal and professional goals. Learn to say no when necessary and avoid spreading oneself too thin.

Setting Boundaries: A Vital Aspect of Maintaining Balance

Boundaries are crucial not only in separating work from personal life but also in protecting one's mental and emotional well-being. In high society, boundaries are often tested due to the constant demand for one's time and attention. Here's how to establish and maintain these boundaries effectively.

1. Identify Personal Limits

To set boundaries, one must first identify their personal limits. This involves recognizing what is acceptable and what is not in terms of time, energy, and emotional investment. By understanding these limits, individuals can communicate them more effectively to others.

2. Communicate Clearly

Clear communication is key to setting and maintaining boundaries. High society often involves social interactions where indirect communication is prevalent. However, it's crucial to be clear and assertive when expressing one's limits and expectations. This ensures that others understand and respect these boundaries.

3. Learn to Say No

Saying no can be challenging, especially in high society where social obligations can feel obligatory. Nevertheless, it is important to say no when a commitment does not align with one's priorities or well-being. Remember that saying no is not a sign of weakness but a demonstration of self-respect and the protection of one's personal space.

4. Seek Support

Seeking support from trusted friends, family, or professionals can be invaluable in maintaining boundaries. Discuss your struggles and concerns with those you trust, and seek advice on how to handle challenging situations. Their perspective and guidance can help you navigate the complexities of high society with greater ease.

Pursuing Passions Beyond Material Pursuits

In high society, the pursuit of material success and social status often takes center stage. While these pursuits are important, it's equally crucial to explore passions and interests that go beyond the material realm. This not only adds depth and meaning to life but also contributes to a more balanced existence.

1. Define Personal Passions

Discovering one's passions is a journey of self-discovery. It involves exploring different activities and interests to identify what truly ignites one's enthusiasm. Whether it's art, music, sports, or philanthropy, high society individuals should invest time in uncovering and nurturing their personal passions.

2. Allocate Time for Hobbies

Once personal passions are identified, allocate time in your schedule to pursue them regularly. High society can be all-consuming, but it's essential to make time for activities that bring joy and fulfillment. Engaging in hobbies provides a much-needed break from the demands of high society and contributes to overall well-being.

3. Connect with Like-Minded Individuals

High society often connects individuals with a vast network of influential people. Leverage this network to find like-minded individuals who share your passions. Engaging with individuals who have similar interests can lead to meaningful connections and collaborations that add depth and purpose to one's life.

4. Balance Material and Non-Material Pursuits

While material success is an integral part of high society, it should not be the sole focus. Balance is achieved by combining material pursuits with non-material ones. Consider how your financial success can enable you to pursue your passions and make a positive impact on the world. This synergy creates a more fulfilling and balanced lifestyle.

The Role of Mentorship and Guidance

Navigating the complexities of high society can be challenging, and it's beneficial to seek mentorship and guidance from experienced individuals who have successfully balanced their lives in this realm. Mentorship provides valuable insights and support, helping one make informed decisions and overcome obstacles.

1. Identify a Mentor

Identifying a mentor within high society circles can be immensely beneficial. A mentor can offer guidance on managing work-life balance, setting boundaries, and pursuing passions, drawing from their own experiences. Look for someone whose values align with your own and who is willing to provide support and advice.

2. Seek Mentorship for Specific Goals

Mentorship doesn't have to be limited to a single individual. Depending on your goals, seek out multiple mentors who specialize in different areas. For example, one mentor might guide you on professional success, while another can offer insights into maintaining a balanced personal life.

3. Foster Meaningful Connections

Mentorship is not just about gaining knowledge; it's also about fostering meaningful connections. Build strong relationships with your mentors, as these relationships can be a source of emotional support and encouragement during challenging times.

Conclusion

Living in high society is a unique and often demanding experience. Achieving a balanced lifestyle within this world is not only possible but essential for overall well-being and success. By prioritizing self-care, setting boundaries, pursuing passions beyond material pursuits, and seeking mentorship and guidance, individuals in high society can navigate its challenges with grace and fulfillment.

In a world where success is often measured by material wealth and social status, remember that true success is also defined by the quality of your personal and professional life. Striking a balance between work and personal life, setting and maintaining boundaries, and pursuing passions beyond material pursuits are key steps towards achieving a fulfilling and balanced lifestyle in high society.

"Navigating Challenges in High Society" takes readers on a thought-provoking journey through the intricate world of high-class society, shedding light on the unique issues and dilemmas faced by its members. From the widening wealth gap to the perils of materialism, social isolation, and the environmental repercussions of lavish living, this book delves into the multifaceted challenges that high-class individuals confront.

It explores the pressures, expectations, and mental health struggles that accompany privilege, while also offering solutions. With chapters covering family dynamics, ethical considerations, and the redefinition of success, this book provides a comprehensive guide to living a more meaningful and sustainable life within high society. Ultimately, it advocates for a balanced, mindful, and socially responsible approach to navigating the world of privilege and influence.

ABOUT THE AUTHOR

Mr. C. P. Kumar is a retired Scientist 'G' from National Institute of Hydrology, Roorkee, Uttarakhand, India. He is also a Reiki Healer and Chakra Balancing practitioner (with pendulum dowsing) and offers Emotional Freedom Technique (EFT) to help individuals with emotional issues. Mr. Kumar has authored many books on technical, spiritual, and social topics.

For further details, you may visit his webpage
https://www.angelfire.com/nh/cpkumar/virgo.html